Adobe Prem_ 2025 User Guide for Beginners

A Step-by-Step Manual to Mastering Video Editing with Latest Tools and Features

Abigail Yosef

Table of Contents

Chapter 1

Getting Started with Adobe Premiere Pro 2025

System Requirements

Before jumping into video editing, it's essential to make sure your computer meets the necessary specs to run Adobe Premiere Pro 2025 smoothly. With each new update, Premiere Pro becomes more powerful—and as a result, it also becomes more demanding on your system.

Basic System Requirements:

- **Operating System:** Windows 10 (64-bit) version 22H2 or newer / macOS 12 Monterey or newer
- **Processor:** Intel® 7th generation or later, or AMD with SSE4.1 support
- **Memory (RAM):** Minimum 16 GB (32 GB or more recommended for 4K editing)
- **Graphics:** At least 4 GB of GPU VRAM (6 GB or more for optimal performance)
- **Storage:** 8 GB of free space for installation; SSDs are strongly advised for editing and cache storage
- **Display Resolution:** Minimum 1920 x 1080

Tips for Optimal Performance:

- Regularly update your graphics drivers

- Close unused apps to free up memory
- Store your media and cache files on an SSD for faster processing

Installing and Setting Up Premiere Pro

Step 1: Download and Install

- Head over to the Adobe Creative Cloud website
- Log in or sign up for an Adobe account
- Locate **Premiere Pro** under the Apps section and click **Install**

Step 2: First-Time Setup

- Once installed, open Premiere Pro via the Creative Cloud app or from your desktop
- The first time you run it, the software might prompt you to install extra files like codecs or fonts—go ahead and approve these

Step 3: Customize Preferences (Optional but Recommended)

- Navigate to **Edit > Preferences** on Windows or **Premiere Pro > Preferences** on macOS
- Adjust key settings such as:
- **Media Cache** (set to an SSD if possible)
- **Auto Save** frequency
- **Theme appearance** (light or dark mode to suit your preference)

Fine-tuning these preferences early on can make your editing experience smoother and more efficient.

Exploring the Welcome Screen

When you launch Premiere Pro, you'll be greeted by the **Welcome Screen**—your main control center for starting or continuing projects.

Here's what you'll find:

- **Home Tab:** View recent projects, start a new one, or open an existing project
- **Learn Tab:** Access a collection of tutorials and guided lessons tailored for beginners
- **New Project Button:** Kick off a fresh project setup
- **Open Project Button:** Browse and open saved Premiere Pro files
- **Templates (New in 2025):** Choose from ready-made templates for platforms like YouTube, TikTok, Instagram Reels, and business videos—perfect for getting started quickly

Spend a little time exploring these features. As you grow more comfortable, navigating through Premiere Pro will become second nature.

Chapter 2

Understanding the Interface

Becoming comfortable with the interface of Adobe Premiere Pro is a key step to editing with confidence. While it might appear overwhelming at first, the software's layout is intentionally designed to keep all the necessary tools within easy reach. Let's take a look at the workspace to make navigating it easier for you.

Workspaces Overview

Premiere Pro 2025 is divided into **Workspaces**, which are pre-configured layouts designed for specific editing tasks like video editing, color correction, audio mixing, and more.

Key Default Workspaces:

- **Editing:** The standard layout, ideal for assembling and editing your project.
- **Color:** Focused on color grading and correction, featuring the Lumetri Color panel.
- **Audio:** Tailored for sound editing, effects adjustments, and mixing.
- **Effects:** For applying video effects, transitions, and working with keyframes.
- **Graphics:** Best for working on text, titles, and motion graphics.

- **Assembly & Review:** A simplified view for managing and reviewing your media.

You can easily switch between these workspaces at the top of the screen or by selecting **Window > Workspaces**. If you've moved or closed a panel and want to return to the default layout, go to **Window > Workspaces > Reset to Saved Layout**.

Panels and Their Functions

Premiere Pro's interface is made up of several panels, each designed to handle specific tasks. Understanding their functions will help you become more efficient in your editing process.

Important Panels Include:

- **Project Panel:** This is your media library, where you import, organize, and preview clips.
- **Source Monitor:** Previews raw clips before adding them to the timeline.
- **Timeline Panel:** The main area for editing, where you assemble your video sequence.
- **Program Monitor:** Shows a real-time preview of your timeline, displaying your project as it progresses.
- **Tools Panel:** Contains editing tools like the Razor, Selection, and Hand tool.
- **Effects Panel:** The place to find video and audio effects, along with transitions.
- **Effect Controls:** Used to modify and animate properties of the clips you select.

- **Audio Meters:** Monitors the audio levels, ensuring proper sound quality throughout your project.

You can move, resize, dock, or undock these panels based on your personal workflow needs.

Customizing Your Workspace

As you become more experienced, you may feel that the default workspace doesn't perfectly suit your editing style. Fortunately, Premiere Pro allows you to customize the layout to match your preferences.

How to Customize:

- Drag panels to reposition them.
- Resize panels by dragging their borders.
- Dock panels into existing groups for a cleaner layout.
- Close unused panels to reduce clutter and focus on what matters.

Saving Your Custom Layout:

Once you've arranged your workspace to your liking, go to **Window > Workspaces > Save as New Workspace**. Give your custom layout a name (e.g., "My Editing Setup") and save it. To return to or switch between layouts later, simply go back to the **Workspaces** menu.

By creating a personalized workspace, you can streamline your editing process and stay organized, especially when working on larger or more complex projects.

Chapter 3

Starting a New Project

When you're ready to start editing, the first step is to set up your project in Adobe Premiere Pro. This involves creating a new project file, adjusting the settings to fit your preferences, and understanding how to manage where your project's media and storage files are kept. Let's go through the process step by step.

Creating a New Project

To initiate a new project in Premiere Pro, follow these steps:

1. Open Premiere Pro and navigate to the **Welcome Screen**.
2. Click on the **New Project** button.
3. A window will appear asking you to name your project and select a storage location.

- **Project Name:** Choose a descriptive name that makes it easy to identify your project.
- **Location:** Select a folder on your computer or an external drive where the project file will be saved. It's recommended to create a separate folder for each project to keep everything organized.

After filling in the details, click **OK** to create your project. You'll be taken to the editing workspace, where you can start importing media and working on your timeline.

Setting Project Preferences

Before you begin editing, it's important to adjust your project settings to match your editing style and system. Here's how to do it:

1. Navigate to **File > Project Settings > General**.
2. **Select the Video Renderer:** Depending on your hardware, you may want to choose a video renderer (e.g., Mercury Playback Engine). The default setting works for most users, but for higher performance, select the appropriate option.
3. **Capture Format (if needed):** If you plan to use hardware capture, select the device or format that fits your needs. This is typically only necessary for specialized workflows.

Other Key Preferences:

- **Auto Save:** Set the frequency for automatic saves (usually every 5-10 minutes). This feature is a lifesaver if Premiere Pro crashes unexpectedly.
- **Timecode Format:** Choose the timecode format (e.g., frames, feet, or meters) based on what your project requires.

Customizing your preferences helps streamline the editing process and prevents unnecessary changes later on.

Understanding Scratch Disks

Scratch Disks are temporary storage areas that Premiere Pro uses during editing. These disks store media cache files, preview files, and other temporary data that enhance performance.

By default, Premiere Pro stores these files on your system drive (usually **C:** on Windows or **Macintosh HD** on macOS). However, it's better to store them on a faster drive, like an SSD, to avoid slowdowns.

To set up your Scratch Disks:

1. Go to **File > Project Settings > Scratch Disks**.
2. You'll be prompted to specify storage locations for different types of files:

- Captured Video
- Captured Audio
- Video Previews
- Audio Previews

It's a good idea to assign these files to a separate, faster drive if you can. This improves playback and rendering speeds, especially for large projects.

By configuring your Scratch Disks properly, you ensure that Premiere Pro runs efficiently without filling up your main storage.

With your project created, preferences adjusted, and Scratch Disks set up, you're ready to start importing media and editing your first sequence. Staying organized from the start will save you time and effort down the line.

Chapter 4

Importing Media

To begin editing, the first step is to bring your media into Premiere Pro. Properly importing your video, audio, and image files is crucial for setting up your project efficiently. This chapter will walk you through the process of importing your media, keeping it organized, and using the Media Browser to make the task easier.

Importing Video, Audio, and Images

Premiere Pro allows you to easily import various types of media, including video clips, audio files, and images. Here's how to import each:

1. **Importing Video Clips:**

   - Go to **File > Import** or press **Ctrl+I** (Windows) or **Cmd+I** (Mac).
   - Navigate to the folder containing your video files, select the clips you want to import, and click **Open**.
   - Your video clips will now appear in the **Project Panel**, ready to be added to your timeline.

2. **Importing Audio Files:**

   - Follow the same process as video import. You can bring in audio files such as **WAV** or **MP3**.

17

- Audio files will be displayed in the **Project Panel** under the **Audio** section.

3. **Importing Images:**

- You can import images the same way as video and audio files.
- Images are usually imported as static files, but you can animate or incorporate them in motion graphics.

Drag-and-Drop   Method:
You can also drag and drop your media directly from your file explorer into the **Project Panel** for a faster import process.

Organizing Media in the Project Panel

Once imported, organizing your media is essential for efficient editing. Premiere Pro offers several tools to help you manage your files in the **Project Panel:**

1. **Creating Folders (Bins):**

- Right-click in the **Project Panel** and select **New Bin**. Bins act like folders, allowing you to categorize your files. You might create bins for **Footage**, **Audio**, **Images**, and **Graphics**.
- Drag and drop files into the appropriate bin to stay organized.

2. **Label Colors:**

- Premiere Pro lets you assign colors to files for easier identification. Right-click on a file, choose **Label**, and pick a color. This helps distinguish between types of media (e.g., red for video clips, blue for audio).

3. **Renaming Files:**

- To rename a file, right-click and select **Rename**. Giving files clear, descriptive names makes it easier to locate them later.

4. **Sorting Files:**

- You can sort files in the **Project Panel** by clicking on column headers such as **Name**, **Type**, or **Date Modified**. Sorting by name is the most common, but you can adjust it to fit your project's needs.

By keeping your media well-organized in the **Project Panel**, you'll save time and stay on top of your project.

Using the Media Browser

The **Media Browser** is a powerful tool that allows you to browse and import media directly from your computer or external drives. It's particularly useful for managing files stored in multiple locations.

1. **Opening the Media Browser:**

- Go to **Window > Media Browser** to open the panel.

2. **Navigating Your Files:**

- The **Media Browser** helps you browse through your file system and preview media files before importing. This is useful for quickly finding clips without opening a separate file explorer.

3. **Previewing Media:**

- Click on any file in the **Media Browser** to preview it. This allows you to check the file before importing it into your project.

4. **Importing from the Media Browser:**

- To import a file, right-click and select **Import**, or drag the file directly into the **Project Panel**.

5. **Handling Different Media Formats:**

- The **Media Browser** supports multiple formats, including video, audio, images, and even sequences from other Premiere Pro projects.

Using the **Media Browser** streamlines the process of locating and importing media, especially for projects with a lot of footage.

Once your media is imported and properly organized, you're ready to dive into editing. Keeping your files neat and easily accessible ensures a smoother, more efficient workflow throughout your project.

Chapter 5

Managing Your Media Assets

Efficiently managing and organizing your media assets is essential for maintaining a smooth editing workflow. This chapter covers how to use bins for organization, leverage metadata and labels to track assets, and implement best practices for a tidy and well-structured project.

Creating and Using Bins

Bins in Premiere Pro serve as organizational folders for your media files. Properly utilizing bins will help you stay organized, especially in large projects with many files.

1. **Creating Bins:**

- Right-click in the **Project Panel** and choose **New Bin** to create a bin.
- Name the bins based on the type of media they hold, such as **Footage**, **Audio**, **Images**, and **Graphics**.
- You can create **sub-bins** within a main bin by right-clicking on an existing bin and selecting **New Bin**, which is especially useful for more complex projects.

2. **Moving Files into Bins:**

- After setting up bins, drag and drop your media into the appropriate bins to keep things organized and make finding files easier.

3. **Organizing Files Within Bins:**

- Sort the contents of each bin by clicking on column headers like **Name**, **Type**, or **Date Modified** to quickly find what you need.

Bins are an effective way to organize and locate media quickly, helping you save time during the editing process.

Best Practices for Organization

Efficient organization is the backbone of smooth editing, especially for large or complex projects. Follow these best practices to keep your media assets well-organized:

1. **Start with a Structured Folder System:**

- Before importing media into Premiere Pro, create a folder structure on your computer or external drive (e.g., **Footage**, **Audio**, **Graphics**, **Project Files**).
- This structure will ensure you can easily find the files you need when you import them into Premiere Pro.

2. **Use Descriptive File Names:**

- Always use clear, descriptive names for your files (e.g., **Scene_01_Take_02.mp4**) to make it easier to find specific clips during editing.

3. **Organize Assets Early:**

- As soon as you import your media, place it into the appropriate bins and apply labels where necessary. Starting your project with a solid organization plan will save time and avoid confusion as the project progresses.

4. **Keep Backup Copies:**

- Always back up your media and project files to avoid losing work due to data corruption or accidental deletions.

5. **Regularly Clean Your Media:**

- As your project evolves, you'll accumulate unused files. Periodically review your bins and delete or archive files that are no longer necessary to keep your workspace uncluttered.

Chapter 6

Navigating the Timeline

The Timeline is where the core of your editing work takes place. Learning to navigate it efficiently is essential for a smooth and quick editing process. In this chapter, we'll go over the key components of timeline tracks, zooming and scrolling techniques, and how to use markers and timecodes to stay organized.

Understanding Tracks

The Timeline in Premiere Pro is divided into several tracks where you place and arrange your media. These tracks are where you'll construct your sequence, and understanding their roles will help you manage even complex projects.

1. **Video Tracks:**

   - Video tracks are used for placing video clips, graphics, and other visual elements. The higher the track, the more it will appear in the foreground.
   - For example, a clip placed on **Video 2** will overlay a clip on **Video 1**.

2. **Audio Tracks:**

   - Audio tracks are for sound elements like dialogue, music, and sound effects. Just like video tracks, audio tracks come in layers and can be adjusted in volume or placement.

- These tracks are labeled as **Audio 1**, **Audio 2**, etc., and you can have as many as your project needs.

3. **Track Controls:**

- Each track has controls for muting, soloing, locking, or hiding the track. These controls are located to the left of the timeline.
- **Locking** a track prevents any changes to its media, while **muting** silences its audio during playback.

4. **Track Height:**

- You can adjust the height of both video and audio tracks by dragging their borders. Increasing the track height can be helpful for detailed edits and working with smaller clips.

Zooming and Scrolling Techniques

Mastering the zooming and scrolling functions is key to fine-tuning your edits and keeping your timeline well-organized.

1. **Zooming In and Out:**

- Use the **Zoom Bar** at the bottom of the timeline to zoom in or out. Zooming in allows you to see more detail, while zooming out gives you a broader view of your sequence.

- You can also hold **Alt** (Windows) or **Option** (Mac) and scroll with the mouse wheel to zoom in and out.

2. **Scrolling:**

- To scroll horizontally, drag the scroll bar at the bottom of the timeline, or hold **Shift** while scrolling with the mouse wheel.
- To scroll vertically (if using multiple tracks), use the regular mouse wheel or the vertical scrollbar on the right side of the timeline.
- Combining zooming and scrolling will help you navigate your project efficiently.

Timeline Markers and Timecodes

Markers and timecodes are invaluable for keeping track of specific moments in your project, ensuring precision when making edits, especially in larger projects.

1. **Timecodes:**

- Timecodes indicate the precise location of a frame in your video, typically in the format **hh:mm:ss:ff** (hours:minutes:seconds:frames).
- The **timecode display** at the bottom of the Program Monitor shows the current position in your sequence, which is useful for syncing clips or pinpointing key moments for edits.

2. **Timeline Markers:**

- Markers are visual cues that you place at specific points on your timeline. They help you note important moments such as scene changes, edits, or sync points.
- To add a marker, press **M** while the playhead is at the desired point, or right-click the timeline and choose **Add Marker**.
- Markers can be renamed and color-coded for easy identification and context.

3. **Using Markers for Organization:**

- Markers are also useful for organization. You can place them to highlight areas where you want to add transitions, effects, or other adjustments later.
- If you're working with audio, markers are especially helpful for syncing sound effects or dialogue with corresponding video clips.

Chapter 7

Basic Editing Techniques

This chapter covers essential video editing techniques in Adobe Premiere Pro. Whether you're cutting, trimming, or rearranging clips, mastering these fundamental tools will help you create a polished and professional project.

Cutting and Trimming Clips

Cutting and trimming are vital techniques for removing unwanted sections of your video or adjusting clip timing.

1. **Cutting Clips:**

   - Use the **Razor Tool** (C) to split your clips into separate parts. Simply click on the timeline at the point where you want to cut. Once split, the clips become individual elements that you can move, delete, or modify independently.
   - Alternatively, place the **playhead** where you want to cut and press **Ctrl+K** (Windows) or **Cmd+K** (Mac) to make the cut.

2. **Trimming Clips:**

   - Trimming allows you to adjust the beginning and end of a clip, either shortening or lengthening its duration. To trim, hover over the clip's edge in the timeline until you see a red **trim cursor** (a bracket with an arrow).

- Drag the clip's edge to adjust its duration. Hold **Alt** (Windows) or **Option** (Mac) while trimming to enable **ripple trimming**, which automatically shifts adjacent clips to maintain timeline continuity.

Ripple, Roll, Slip, and Slide Edits

These four editing tools provide advanced control for manipulating clips, giving you more flexibility in your workflow.

1. **Ripple Edit:**

- The **Ripple Edit Tool** (B) adjusts the in or out point of a clip, and automatically moves the following clips in the timeline to maintain the sequence's structure. It's especially useful for speeding up or slowing down a sequence without causing gaps or disturbing the timing.

2. **Roll Edit:**

- The **Roll Edit Tool** (N) changes the cut point between two clips. This tool moves the in point of the next clip and the out point of the previous clip, keeping the total sequence duration unchanged.
- It's ideal for refining transitions between clips without impacting the surrounding timeline.

3. **Slip Edit:**

- The **Slip Edit Tool** (Y) modifies the in and out points of a clip at the same time, effectively altering the visible portion of the clip while keeping its position in the timeline intact. This is useful when you need to adjust the timing of a clip but don't want to move it.

4. **Slide Edit:**

- The **Slide Edit Tool** (U) moves a clip within the timeline, while simultaneously adjusting the in and out points of neighboring clips to fit the change. It's great for repositioning clips and maintaining the flow of your sequence.

Rearranging Clips in the Timeline

Rearranging clips helps you restructure your footage and create new sequences. There are several ways to reposition clips in the timeline.

1. **Drag-and-Drop:**

- To move a clip, click on it in the timeline, hold the mouse button, and drag it to a new location. Premiere Pro will automatically adjust the positions of adjacent clips to accommodate the change.

2. **Using Arrow Keys:**

- Select a clip and use the **Left Arrow** or **Right Arrow** keys to move it one frame at a time. This is useful for making precise adjustments without affecting the overall timing.

3. **Ripple Move:**

- Using the **Ripple Edit Tool**, you can move a clip in the timeline, and Premiere Pro will automatically adjust surrounding clips to fill any gaps, ensuring your sequence stays intact.

Chapter 8

Working with Audio

Adjusting Volume and Gain

Adjusting the volume and gain of audio clips is crucial in video editing to maintain clear and balanced sound throughout your project. Proper adjustments help avoid issues like distorted audio or inconsistent sound levels.

Adjusting Volume

1. **In the Timeline:**

- Select the audio clip on the timeline.
- Hover over the **volume line** (the horizontal line in the audio track) until your cursor becomes a **pen tool**.
- Click and drag the line up or down to increase or decrease the clip's volume.
- You can also set multiple **keyframes** along the line to adjust the volume dynamically, such as creating fade-ins or fade-outs.

2. **Using the Audio Mixer:**

- Open the **Audio Mixer** from Window > Audio Mixer.
- Locate the track for your audio clip and adjust the **fader** to control the volume.

3. **Clip Gain:**

- Right-click the audio clip and choose **Audio Gain**.
- In the **Audio Gain** window, enter a specific value to increase or decrease the gain, which adjusts the overall loudness of the clip without changing other settings.

Adjusting Gain

1. **Clip Gain in the Timeline:**

- Right-click on the clip in the timeline and select **Audio Gain**.
- In the window that appears, you can adjust the gain value by entering a number for increase or decrease, or by normalizing the gain to a specific peak level (e.g., Normalize Max Peak to -3 dB).

2. **Normalize Audio:**

- Alternatively, you can normalize the audio by selecting the clip and going to **Clip > Audio Options > Normalize Audio**.
- This option automatically adjusts the clip's volume to the maximum peak level or to a specific decibel setting of your choice.

Applying Audio Transitions

Audio transitions are used to create smooth shifts between audio clips, such as fading in and out or merging two clips seamlessly. These transitions are important for maintaining a smooth audio experience and avoiding abrupt audio changes that can disrupt the flow.

Adding an Audio Transition

Using the Effects Panel:

- Open the **Effects** panel (Window > Effects).
- Inside the **Audio Transitions** section, you'll find common effects like **Constant Power**, **Constant Gain**, and **Exponential Fade**.
- Drag your chosen transition to the point where two audio clips meet on the timeline.

Adjusting the Transition:

- After applying the transition, adjust its duration by dragging the edges of the transition icon in the timeline.
- For a smoother transition, experiment with different types (e.g., **Constant Power** for a smooth fade), depending on the effect you're aiming for.

Customizing the Transition:

- Once applied, you can modify the transition by selecting it in the timeline and adjusting its settings in the **Effect Controls** panel. This lets you refine the transition's length and style to match your needs.

Removing a Transition:

- To remove a transition, simply select it in the timeline and press **Delete** or drag it off the timeline.

Audio transitions are key to maintaining smooth and natural audio flow, particularly when moving between different clips like dialogue, sound effects, or music.

Overview of the Audio Track Mixer

The Audio Track Mixer in Adobe Premiere Pro offers a more advanced and precise method for controlling and mixing audio levels across various tracks in your project. It provides real-time adjustments and a more intuitive workflow for refining audio during editing.

Accessing the Audio Track Mixer:

To open the Audio Track Mixer, navigate to **Window > Audio Track Mixer**.

The mixer will display a vertical fader for each audio track in your timeline, giving you the ability to adjust the volume of each track individually.

Main Features:

1. **Volume Faders:**

- Each track in the Audio Track Mixer has a volume fader, allowing you to adjust the overall volume of the track in real time.

- You can use these faders to balance the audio levels of different elements, like dialogue, music, and sound effects.

2. **Pan Control:**

- Positioned next to each volume fader is the **Pan** control, which lets you position the audio in the left or right channel (stereo panning). This helps create a more immersive and dynamic audio experience.

3. **Mute and Solo Buttons:**

- The **Mute** button silences a track temporarily without deleting it, which is useful for isolating other tracks while editing.
- The **Solo** button mutes all tracks except the selected one, ideal when you need to focus on a particular audio element.

4. **Track Effects:**

- You can apply audio effects directly to tracks within the Audio Track Mixer, allowing you to enhance the sound of entire tracks with effects like reverb, EQ, and compression.

5. **Automation:**

- The Audio Track Mixer supports **automation**, meaning you can set keyframes to adjust audio levels and other parameters over time. This is especially helpful for changes like fading out music while keeping dialogue clear.

6. **Recording:**

- The mixer also provides recording options, allowing you to capture live adjustments to audio or record voiceovers directly within Premiere Pro.

Chapter 9

Adding Transitions and Effects

Using Video Transitions

Video transitions help create smooth, seamless changes between clips, enhancing the flow of your video. Whether you're transitioning between scenes, shots, or video elements, these transitions add a polished, professional touch and can make your edits more dynamic.

Adding a Video Transition:

1. **Using the Effects Panel:**

   - Access the **Effects** panel by going to **Window > Effects**.
   - In the **Video Transitions** folder, you'll find a range of options like **Dissolve**, **Wipe**, **Slide**, and **Zoom**.
   - Drag the desired transition effect to the point where two clips meet on the timeline.

2. **Adjusting the Transition:**

   - After applying the transition, you can adjust its duration by dragging its edges along the timeline.
   - For finer control over the transition, modify its properties in the **Effect Controls** panel to tweak its timing and smoothness.

Customizing the Transition:

- Click on the transition in the timeline and open the **Effect Controls** panel to adjust its settings.
- Some transitions allow you to modify the direction, speed, and shape, offering more creative control over how the transition appears.

Removing a Transition:

- To remove a transition, select it in the timeline and press **Delete**, or simply drag it out of the timeline.

Types of Video Transitions:

- **Dissolve**: These transitions create a gradual fade between clips, with **Cross Dissolve** being the most widely used.
- **Wipes**: A wipe transition replaces one clip with another by "wiping" across the screen in a specific direction.
- **Slides**: These transitions slide one clip off-screen, making space for the next clip.
- **Zoom**: These create a zoom effect that visually moves the viewer into the next shot or scene.

Tips for Using Transitions:

- Use transitions sparingly to avoid overwhelming your content. Apply them strategically to highlight important moments or enhance scene changes.

- Ensure the transitions match the tone and style of your video. For example, a fast **Zoom** transition suits action sequences, while a **Cross Dissolve** is ideal for smoother, more subtle scene transitions.

Applying Video Effects

Video effects are tools that enhance, modify, or add creative elements to your footage. Whether you're adjusting colors, improving visuals, or creating stylistic touches, video effects can greatly transform your project. This section covers how to apply video effects to clips and adjust them to achieve your desired result.

Adding Video Effects:

1. **Using the Effects Panel:**

- Open the **Effects** panel by selecting **Window > Effects**.
- Inside the **Video Effects** folder, you'll find various categories, including **Color Correction**, **Blur & Sharpen**, **Distort**, **Transform**, and more.
- Drag the desired effect from the panel and drop it onto the video clip in the timeline.

Adjusting Video Effects:

- After applying an effect, navigate to the **Effect Controls** panel to tweak its settings.
- You can modify various properties of the effect, such as intensity, scale, position, or color adjustments, depending on the effect applied.

Customizing Video Effects:

- In the **Effect Controls** panel, each effect comes with its own set of customizable properties. For instance, if you apply a **Gaussian Blur**, you can adjust the blur amount to soften or sharpen the image.
- Some effects, such as **Keying** or **Chroma Key**, allow for detailed adjustments like fine-tuning thresholds or range.

Animating Effects:

- Many video effects can be animated over time using **keyframes**. This allows you to adjust the effect's properties at specific points within the timeline.
- For example, you can gradually increase the intensity of a **brightness and contrast** effect or animate the position of an image over time.

Removing or Replacing Video Effects:

- To remove an effect, go to the **Effect Controls** panel, select the effect, and click the **Delete** button or press **Delete** on your keyboard.
- To replace an effect, simply drag a new effect from the **Effects** panel and drop it on the clip, overwriting the existing one.

Types of Common Video Effects:

- **Color Correction**: Modify color balance, brightness, contrast, and saturation of your footage.
- **Blur**: Softens the image for artistic effects or to create focus.
- **Distort**: Changes the video's shape or structure, such as with **Warp** or **Transform** effects.
- **Keying**: Removes a specific color range, often used for **green screen** effects.
- **Stylize**: Applies artistic filters to give your footage a unique look, such as **Cartoon** or **Invert** effects.

Tips for Applying Video Effects:

- Begin with subtle effects, especially for **color correction**. Overusing effects can be distracting.
- Use the **Effect Controls** panel for precise adjustments and live previews.
- Experiment with different effects to discover which best suits the style and tone of your project.

The **Effect Controls Panel** in Premiere Pro is a central workspace for adjusting and fine-tuning both video and audio effects applied to your clips. It offers precise control over various properties, allowing you to modify effects, animate them over time, and manage keyframes. Here's how to use it:

Overview of the Effect Controls Panel:

- **Location:**
  To access the **Effect Controls Panel**, navigate to **Window > Effect Controls**.

- **Panel   Layout:**
  The panel shows all applied effects for the selected clip, including both video and audio, along with their corresponding properties and keyframes. Effects are listed in the order they were applied, and each effect has adjustable settings.

Key Features of the Effect Controls Panel:

Motion   Controls:
The **Motion** section lets you adjust a clip's **position**, **scale**, **rotation**, and **anchor point**. You can animate these properties by setting keyframes.

- **Position:** Controls the clip's placement on screen.
- **Scale:** Adjusts the clip's size.
- **Rotation:** Allows you to rotate the clip.
- **Anchor Point:** Defines the pivot point for transformations.

Opacity:
The **Opacity** section allows you to control the clip's transparency. You can adjust the opacity and animate the fade in or out of the clip using keyframes.

- **Audio   Effects:**
  If audio effects are applied, they will appear under the **Audio Effects** section, where you can adjust settings like volume, panning, and other audio parameters.
- **Applied   Video   Effects:**
  The **Video Effects** section shows all applied video effects, such as color correction, blur, or

keying. Each effect has properties that can be customized.

- **Keyframes:**
The **Effect Controls Panel** enables you to animate effects by using keyframes. A keyframe marks a specific time where a change occurs, such as moving a clip's position from one side of the screen to another.

To add a keyframe, click the stopwatch icon next to the effect property, then move the playhead to another point in the timeline and modify the property's value. Premiere Pro will automatically create a new keyframe.

- **Resetting   Effects:**
To remove all changes to a specific effect, right-click on the effect and select **Reset**.
- **Effect   Presets:**
The **Effect Controls Panel** also lets you save your customized settings as presets, which can be applied to other clips in the project to maintain consistency.

Using the Effect Controls Panel:

- To modify an effect, first select the clip in the timeline, then open the **Effect Controls Panel**.
- Expand the desired effect section by clicking the dropdown arrow next to its name. From there, you can adjust properties or animate the effect.
- To apply a new effect, simply drag it from the **Effects Panel** to the clip in the **Effect Controls Panel**.

Tips for Using the Effect Controls Panel:

- **Organize   Effects:**
  Group similar effects together, such as placing all color correction effects in one section and audio effects in another.
- **Preview   Changes:**
  Use the program monitor to view real-time changes as you make adjustments in the **Effect Controls Panel**.
- **Animate   Smoothly:**
  For fluid animation, use ease-in and ease-out keyframes, ensuring smoother transitions.

The **Effect Controls Panel** is a vital tool for precise editing, allowing you to create the perfect visual and audio effects for your project.

Chapter 10

Using the Essential Graphics Panel

Adding Titles and Text

In video editing, titles and text play a crucial role in delivering information, enhancing the narrative, or providing a polished, professional feel. Premiere Pro offers a variety of tools to help you create and personalize text for your video projects. Here's a guide on how to incorporate titles and text into your work:

Creating a Simple Title:

- **Using the Type Tool:**
  1. Select the **Type Tool** (T) from the toolbar or press **T** on your keyboard.
  2. Click anywhere in the **Program Monitor** to add text and begin typing.
  3. The text will appear in the **Essential Graphics** panel, where you can adjust the content, font, size, color, and other attributes.
- **Using the New Title Option:**
  1. Navigate to **File > New > Legacy Title**.
  2. A new window will open, allowing you to type and format your title.
  3. Adjust properties such as font, size, color, and position within the Title panel.

Editing and Customizing Titles:

- **Essential Graphics Panel:** Once you add text using the Type Tool, you can open the **Essential Graphics Panel** (Window > Essential Graphics) to refine your text properties:
- **Font and Size:** Change the style and size of the text.
- **Position and Alignment:** Use alignment tools to adjust where the text appears on screen.
- **Color and Opacity:** Modify the text color and transparency for blending with the background.
- **Stroke and Shadow:** Add a stroke (outline) or drop shadow for emphasis.

Animating Text:

To animate text, use the **Effect Controls Panel** and apply keyframes to properties like position, scale, or opacity over time, creating dynamic motion effects.

Using Pre-Made Templates:

Browse Templates:

1. In the **Essential Graphics Panel**, explore available title templates. Premiere Pro offers various pre-designed templates that can be easily dragged and dropped into your timeline.
2. You can modify the text within these templates using the Essential Graphics Panel.

Importing Templates:

3. You can import title templates from third-party sources or **Adobe Stock** by selecting **Graphics > Browse** and either browsing Adobe Stock or importing custom templates.

Positioning and Aligning Text:

- **Manual Positioning:** Use the **Selection Tool** (V) to drag the text directly in the **Program Monitor** to your preferred position.
- **Auto-Alignment:** In the **Essential Graphics Panel**, align the text by using auto-alignment tools to position it to the left, right, or center of the screen.

Adding Text Animations:

- To animate the text, apply keyframes to adjust properties like position, scale, or opacity over time. For example, you can create a sliding effect by altering the position and adding keyframes.
- **Motion Graphics Templates** (MOGRTs) provide more advanced text animation options, offering pre-designed animations that can be imported and customized.

Finalizing and Adjusting Titles:

- Once your text is ready, you can modify the timing in the timeline by dragging the text clip to the desired position.

- To adjust the **duration** of the title, hover over the clip's edge in the timeline and drag it left or right to fit your needs.

Creating Lower Thirds

Lower thirds are graphic elements typically positioned in the lower third of the screen, used to display information such as names, locations, or other details in a video. Premiere Pro offers versatile tools to design and animate custom lower thirds, providing complete control over their look and movement. Here's how you can create them:

Using Pre-made Templates for Lower Thirds:

1. **Browse Templates:**

- Open the **Essential Graphics Panel** (Window > Essential Graphics).
- Browse through the available pre-made lower third templates, which you can easily drag into your timeline.

2. **Customize the Template:**

- Once the template is added, you can modify the text and its properties (such as font, color, and position) in the **Essential Graphics Panel** to align with your video's style.

3. **Animate the Lower Third:**

- Animate the text and graphics of the lower third by adjusting properties like position, scale, and opacity in the **Effect Controls Panel**.
- Use keyframes to control the timing of animations, such as making the lower third slide in or fade out.

Creating a Custom Lower Third:

1. **Using the Type Tool:**

- Select the **Type Tool** (T) from the toolbar or press **T** on your keyboard.
- Click in the **Program Monitor** where you want the text to appear, and start typing.
- In the **Essential Graphics Panel**, adjust properties like font, size, color, and alignment to create a professional lower third.

2. **Adding Graphics or Shapes:**

- To enhance your lower third, incorporate shapes, lines, or background elements behind the text.
- Use the **Shape Tool** or import images to create a backdrop for the text, ensuring it doesn't overpower the text itself.
- Adjust the position, size, and opacity of these elements as needed.

Positioning the Lower Third:

1. **Manual Positioning:**

- Use the **Selection Tool** (V) to drag and position the text and any additional graphics in the **Program Monitor**.
- Place the lower third in the lower part of the screen for a professional appearance.

2. **Using Auto-Alignment:**

- In the **Essential Graphics Panel**, you can align the text to the left, center, or right to fit your video's style.

Animating Lower Thirds:

1. **Using Keyframes:**

- Open the **Effect Controls Panel** and apply keyframes to animate the text or graphics.
- You can animate the position to make the lower third slide in from the side or adjust the opacity for fade-in/fade-out effects.

2. **Adding Motion Graphics:**

- Use pre-designed **Motion Graphics Templates (MOGRTs)** for more advanced animations.
- Customize these templates to match your project's needs.

Finalizing the Lower Third:

- Adjust the timing in the **Timeline** by selecting the lower third clip and dragging it to the desired position.

- Change the **duration** by dragging the clip's edge in the timeline to the left or right.

Creating custom lower thirds adds a professional touch to your video, making it ideal for displaying names, locations, or additional information. Whether you opt for pre-made templates or create your own, Premiere Pro provides all the necessary tools to make them dynamic and visually striking.

Customizing Fonts and Motion Graphics

Personalizing fonts and adding motion graphics are essential for making your video content visually captivating. Premiere Pro offers a range of tools to customize text and incorporate dynamic motion graphics into your project. Here's how you can customize fonts and create motion graphics:

Customizing Fonts:

1. **Using the Essential Graphics Panel:**

   - Open the **Essential Graphics Panel** (Window > Essential Graphics).
   - Choose the text layer you want to modify in the timeline.
   - In the Essential Graphics Panel, you can adjust various font properties:

     - **Font Style**: Select from available fonts or install custom ones.
     - **Font Size**: Resize the text to fit your design.

- **Font Color**: Modify the text color to match your video's theme.
- **Tracking**: Adjust the space between letters or words.
- **Leading**: Change the spacing between lines of text.
- **Bold, Italic, and Underline**: Apply different text styles for emphasis.

2. **Aligning and Positioning Text:**

- Align the text left, center, or right based on your design.
- Use the **Position** controls in the Essential Graphics Panel to move the text to the desired location.

3. **Adding Text Effects:**

- Enhance your text by adding effects like **stroke**, **drop shadow**, or **glow** for better visibility.
- Modify the **opacity** to either blend the text with the background or create a subtle effect.

Creating Motion Graphics:

Using Motion Graphics Templates (MOGRTs):

- Premiere Pro offers a variety of pre-made **Motion Graphics Templates (MOGRTs)** in the **Essential Graphics Panel**, featuring customizable elements and dynamic animations.
- Simply drag a template to the timeline and modify the text, colors, and timing to suit your project.

- Customize MOGRTs to add animations like fades, slides, and transitions.

Animating Text and Graphics:

1. Select the text or graphic layer in the timeline.
2. Open the **Effect Controls Panel** and use **keyframes** to animate properties like:

   - **Position**: Create movement effects by adjusting the position over time.
   - **Scale**: Animate zoom-in or zoom-out for emphasis.
   - **Opacity**: Add fade-in or fade-out effects.

3. Set keyframes to control the timing and movement of your graphics.

Manually Adding Motion to Text or Graphics:

Adjust properties like **Position, Rotation, Scale**, and **Opacity** in the **Effect Controls Panel** to manually create motion.

- Use keyframes to animate these properties, adding dynamic movement to the text or graphics.

Creating Backgrounds and Overlays:

- Enhance your motion graphics by adding elements like shapes, lines, or color blocks in the background.

- Animate these background elements with keyframes for smooth transitions.
- Use the **Shape Tool** in the Essential Graphics Panel to add shapes or lines, adjusting their opacity and movement during the animation.

Advanced Customization Tips:

- **Use Easing**: Apply **ease-in** and **ease-out** effects on keyframes for smoother transitions in animations.
- **Layering**: Experiment with layering different graphics and text elements to create more complex motion effects, such as having text slide in from one side while a shape enters from the other.
- **Exporting Custom MOGRTs**: After creating a custom motion graphic, save it as a **Motion Graphics Template (MOGRT)** for use in other projects. Simply select "Create MOGRT" in the Essential Graphics Panel.

Finalizing Motion Graphics:

- Once you're satisfied with your fonts and motion graphics, review the animations and adjust their timing to ensure they fit the video's flow.
- Use the **Program Monitor** to preview the motion graphics in real-time as you make adjustments.
- Adjust the duration of the motion graphic clips in the timeline by dragging their edges to set the length of the effect.

Chapter 11

Color Correction and Grading

Using the Lumetri Color Panel

The **Lumetri Color Panel** in Premiere Pro is an essential tool for color grading and correction, providing detailed control over the color, exposure, and contrast of your footage. With this panel, you can improve your project's visual quality, adjust specific color ranges, and achieve professional-level color grading. Here's how to use it effectively:

Opening the Lumetri Color Panel:

1. Navigate to **Window > Lumetri Color** to open the panel.
2. The panel is divided into different sections, each offering specific tools for color correction and grading.

Basic Correction:

The **Basic Correction** section helps correct exposure, white balance, and contrast:

1. **White Balance:**

- Adjust the **Temperature** (warmth) and **Tint** (green to magenta shift) to fix the color balance.

- Use the **Color Picker** to select a neutral area for automatic white balance adjustment.

2. **Tone:**

- **Exposure**: Control the overall brightness.
- **Contrast**: Modify the difference between light and dark areas.
- **Highlights**: Adjust the brightest areas.
- **Shadows**: Tweak the darkest parts of the image.
- **Whites**: Adjust the brightest values.
- **Blacks**: Alter the darkest values, making them deeper or lighter.

3. **Saturation:**

- Increase or decrease the overall color saturation for more vibrant or muted colors.

Creative:

This section is for adding stylistic effects to your footage:

1. **Look:**

- Choose from various **Creative Looks** (presets) to apply specific color grading styles.
- Adjust the intensity of the look as needed.

2. **Faded Film:**

- Apply a faded film effect to reduce contrast and give your footage a vintage, washed-out look.

3. **Sharpen:**

- Enhance or soften the sharpness to highlight finer details or create a smoother appearance.

4. **Vibrance:**

- Increase the intensity of muted colors without oversaturating the already vibrant ones.

Curves:

The **Curves** section allows for precise color adjustments:

1. **RGB Curves:**

- Adjust the **Overall Curve** to manage brightness and contrast.
- Modify the **Red, Green, and Blue curves** separately to fine-tune color balance and correct any color casts.

2. **Hue vs. Hue / Saturation / Luminance Curves:**

- Target specific color ranges and adjust their hue, saturation, or luminance independently. This is especially useful for tweaking colors like the sky or skin tones.

Color Wheels & Match:

The **Color Wheels & Match** section helps balance colors and match clips:

1. **Color Wheels:**

- Adjust the **Shadows**, **Midtones**, and **Highlights** to refine the overall color balance.
- Drag the corresponding wheel to modify colors in the shadows, midtones, or highlights for a stylized effect or color correction.

2. **Color Match:**

- Use this feature to automatically match the color of two clips, ensuring a consistent look across your footage.

HSL Secondary:

The **HSL Secondary** section enables you to adjust specific colors in your footage:

1. **Color Range:**

- Select a color range (e.g., blue skies or skin tones) and use the HSL sliders to adjust the hue, saturation, and luminance of that specific range.

2. **Refine Selection:**

- Fine-tune the color range by adjusting **Range** and **Refine** settings to ensure you only affect the intended area.

Vignette:

The **Vignette** section allows you to apply a vignette effect:

1. **Amount:**

- Adjust how dark or light the vignette effect is.

2. **Midpoint:**

- Control the size of the vignette area.

3. **Roundness:**

- Adjust the shape of the vignette, making it more circular or rectangular.

4. **Feather:**

- Soften the vignette's edges to create a more gradual transition.

Tips for Using the Lumetri Color Panel:

- **Start with Basic Corrections**: Begin by adjusting exposure, contrast, and white balance before moving on to more advanced grading techniques.
- **Use Keyframes for Dynamic Adjustments**: Animate color corrections over time by adding keyframes, such as changing the tone or mood of a scene.
- **Match Shots with Color Wheels**: Use the **Color Match** feature for consistent color across multiple

shots, particularly when switching between different camera angles or lighting setups.

- **Experiment with Curves**: The **Curves** section is excellent for making detailed adjustments to color and contrast, with even small tweaks having a big impact on the overall look.

Basic Color Correction Workflow

Color correction is a crucial part of video editing, ensuring your footage has accurate color balance and proper exposure. This process typically involves adjusting exposure, white balance, and contrast to create a natural and consistent look across your video. Here's a simplified guide to performing basic color correction in Premiere Pro using the Lumetri Color Panel:

1. Set Up the Lumetri Color Panel:

To open the **Lumetri Color Panel**, go to **Window > Lumetri Color**.

This panel includes sections like **Basic Correction**, **Creative**, **Curves**, and **Color Wheels**, which will help you fine-tune your footage's color and exposure.

2. Adjust White Balance:

White balance is essential for ensuring natural colors by removing any color casts caused by lighting conditions.

- **Temperature**: Use the **Temperature** slider to shift the footage towards warmer (yellow) or cooler (blue) tones.

- **Tint**: Fine-tune the **Tint** slider to balance any green or magenta shifts.
- You can also use the **Color Picker** tool in the Basic Correction section to automatically adjust the white balance by selecting a neutral area in your footage.

3. Correct Exposure:

Exposure adjustments are important for avoiding overly bright or dark footage.

- **Exposure**: Adjust the **Exposure** slider to control the image's overall brightness.
- **Contrast**: Use the **Contrast** slider to enhance the difference between light and dark areas.
- **Highlights**: Lower highlights if the bright areas are too intense, or increase them for more detail.
- **Shadows**: Adjust the **Shadows** to reveal details in the darker areas.
- **Whites & Blacks**: Fine-tune the **Whites** and **Blacks** sliders to ensure the brightest and darkest parts are well balanced and not clipped.

4. Adjust Saturation:

Once exposure is corrected, adjust the **Saturation** to control the vibrancy of the colors.

- Increase saturation to make colors pop, or decrease it to create a more subdued look. Ensure the saturation remains natural to avoid oversaturation.

5. Use RGB Curves for Precision:

Curves are useful for precise color and contrast adjustments.

- **RGB Curves**: Manipulate the RGB curve to adjust the overall brightness of the image by raising or lowering the curve.
- **Individual Color Curves**: You can adjust the **Red**, **Green**, and **Blue** curves to correct any color imbalances or color casts (like too much blue or green).

6. Adjust Skin Tones (If Necessary):

For footage with human subjects, it's essential that skin tones look natural.

- Use the **HSL Secondary** section to target and refine skin tones or specific colors in the footage. You can adjust their hue, saturation, and luminance to maintain realistic skin tones.

7. Balance Colors with Color Wheels:

The **Color Wheels** help adjust the color balance of shadows, midtones, and highlights.

- **Shadows**: Modify shadow color to add warmth or coolness to darker areas.
- **Midtones**: Adjust midtones to achieve the desired color balance for the general tone of the footage.
- **Highlights**: Adjust highlight colors to add tints to the brightest areas.

- Ensure the shadows, midtones, and highlights are balanced to avoid unnatural color casts.

8. Add a Vignette:

To focus attention on a particular area, you can apply a vignette.

- **Amount**: Adjust how dark or light the vignette is.
- **Midpoint**: Control the size of the vignette area.
- **Roundness & Feather**: Change the shape of the vignette and soften its edges for a smooth transition.

9. Review Your Adjustments:

After making your adjustments, preview the footage in the **Program Monitor** to ensure the changes look natural. Fine-tune the settings if necessary to achieve the desired look.

10. Final Touches:

Once you're happy with the basic color correction, you can proceed to more advanced color grading or add creative effects using the **Creative** section in the Lumetri Color Panel.

Make sure to save your settings, and if working with multiple clips, apply consistent corrections across all your footage for uniformity.

Creative LUTs and Presets

Creative LUTs (Look-Up Tables) and presets are powerful tools in video editing, allowing you to quickly modify the appearance of your footage by applying color grading or stylistic effects. Premiere Pro includes various built-in LUTs and presets, and you can also import custom ones to achieve unique looks. Here's how to use creative LUTs and presets to enhance your video project:

What are LUTs?

LUTs are formulas that map one set of colors to another, changing the color and tonal properties of your footage. Creative LUTs apply a stylized color grade to your clips, giving them a specific mood or atmosphere, such as cinematic, vintage, or high-contrast effects.

Applying a Creative LUT:

1. **Open the Lumetri Color Panel:**

- Go to **Window > Lumetri Color** to open the Lumetri Color Panel, which contains the Creative section for applying LUTs.

2. **Select the Creative Tab:**

- In the **Lumetri Color Panel**, click the **Creative** tab to access creative LUT options.

3. **Choose a LUT:**

- In the **Look** dropdown menu, browse through the available built-in LUTs in Premiere Pro and select the one you want to apply to your footage.

4. **Adjust Intensity:**

- Use the **Intensity** slider to adjust the strength of the LUT. Move it left to reduce the effect, or right to enhance it.

5. **Fine-tune the Settings:**

- After applying the LUT, you can adjust additional settings like **Exposure, Contrast, Saturation,** and **Vibrance** to perfect the look.

Creating Custom LUTs:

1. **Apply Custom Color Grading:**

- Manually adjust your footage using the **Basic Correction, Curves,** and **Color Wheels** sections of the Lumetri Color Panel to create a custom look.

2. **Export the LUT:**

- Once satisfied with your adjustments, save them as a custom LUT. Click the three lines in the top-right corner of the Lumetri Color Panel and choose **Export .cube** to save the LUT for later use.

3. **Import Custom LUTs:**

- To use your custom LUT, click the **Look** dropdown in the Creative tab and select **Browse** to find and apply the LUT.

Using Creative Presets:

Creative presets are pre-configured color grades or effects that can be quickly applied to your clips.

1. **Browse for Presets:**

   • Find presets in the **Effects** panel under **Presets**. Premiere Pro offers several built-in presets for color grading, transitions, and visual effects.

2. **Apply a Preset:**

   • Drag and drop the chosen preset onto a clip in the timeline to instantly apply the effect or color grade.

3. **Adjust the Preset:**

   • After applying a preset, you can modify its settings in the **Effect Controls** panel to better suit your project. You can tweak the intensity or combine multiple effects for a more custom look.

Working with Third-Party LUTs and Presets:

1. **Import External LUTs and Presets:**

   • You can import third-party LUTs and presets from sources like Adobe Stock or other providers. To do this, go to the **Creative** section, click **Browse**, and locate the files on your computer.

2. **Use LUTs for Quick Grading:**

- LUTs are often used for fast color grading in professional workflows, offering a consistent look or style, such as vintage or cinematic, across multiple clips.

Chapter 12

Working with Keyframes

1. **Understanding** **Keyframe** **Animation**
Keyframes are vital for creating animations in video editing. They allow you to define specific values at set points in time, which enables you to animate various properties such as position, scale, rotation, opacity, and more. Keyframes mark the start and end of an animation, with Premiere Pro automatically generating the transitions between them to create smooth motion.

- **Creating Keyframes**: To create keyframes in Premiere Pro, click the stopwatch icon next to the property you want to animate (e.g., position, scale, opacity). Once the stopwatch is activated, you can move the playhead along the timeline and modify the property's value to set a keyframe at different points.
- **Keyframe Controls**: Each keyframe holds a specific property value at a given moment. As the playhead moves between keyframes, Premiere Pro automatically calculates and generates the motion from one keyframe to the next.

2. **Animating** **Motion** **and** **Opacity**
Animating motion and opacity adds dynamic movement to your video. Here's how to animate different properties:

Animating Motion (Position, Scale, Rotation):

- **Position**: Set keyframes for position to move objects across the screen. For example, to animate a clip from left to right, set a starting keyframe at the beginning of the timeline and another keyframe at the end, where you want the movement to finish.
- **Scale**: Animate the scale of an object or clip to zoom in or out. Set an initial keyframe for scale, then another keyframe later on with a different value.
- **Rotation**: To animate rotation, adjust the rotation property at specific keyframes, enabling spins or other rotational effects.
- **Animating Opacity**: Set keyframes for the opacity property to gradually fade an element in or out. For instance, start with 0% opacity at the beginning and add a keyframe at 100% opacity to make the clip gradually appear.

3.   Smoothing   Keyframe   Transitions
Smoothing transitions between keyframes is essential for creating natural, fluid animations. Here are ways to refine your transitions:

- **Ease In and Ease Out**: Use easing to adjust the speed at the start and end of an animation.
- **Ease In**: Slows down the animation at the beginning for a smooth start.
- **Ease Out**: Slows down the animation at the end for a smooth stop. Right-click on a keyframe in Premiere Pro and select **Ease In** or **Ease Out** to apply these effects.
- **Manual Keyframe Adjustment**: Adjust the speed of an animation by moving keyframes

closer or farther apart. Keyframes that are closer together result in faster motion, while those further apart will slow the animation down.

- **Bezier Curves**: Use Bezier curves for more precise control over keyframe motion. Right-click on a keyframe, choose **Temporal Interpolation > Bezier**, and adjust the curve for finer control over animation speed and timing.

- **Graph Editor**: The Graph Editor in Premiere Pro enables you to view and modify keyframe transitions using curves. By utilizing the **Velocity Graph** or **Value Graph**, you can gain more control over the speed and fluidity of your animations.

Chapter 13

Speed and Time Effects

1. Slow Motion and Fast Motion
Slow motion and fast motion are effective tools for controlling the pace of your video. These effects can draw attention to specific actions, create dramatic moments, or accelerate sequences for a more efficient storytelling pace.

- **Slow Motion:**
  Slow motion is achieved by reducing the speed of the clip, making movements appear more fluid and extended. In Premiere Pro, right-click the clip in the timeline and select **Speed/Duration**. Lower the speed percentage (e.g., setting it to 50% will halve the speed) to achieve the slow-motion effect.

- **Fast Motion:**
  To increase the speed of a clip, use the **Speed/Duration** menu and raise the speed percentage. For example, setting it to 200% will double the speed of the clip. This effect is commonly used for time-lapse sequences or condensing long actions into shorter segments.

2. Time Remapping
Time remapping offers a more flexible approach, enabling you to change the speed of your clip dynamically at different points, creating smooth transitions or variable speed effects.

- **Applying Time Remapping**: Right-click the clip in the timeline, choose **Show Clip Keyframes > Time Remapping > Speed**, and a speed adjustment line will appear across the clip. To modify the speed, click on the line to insert keyframes and adjust them to control the speed at specific points in the clip.
- **Adjusting Keyframes**: By adding and modifying keyframes along the clip, you can change the speed at various moments. This allows for gradual transitions between slow and fast motion, or dramatic time-stretch effects.

3. Reverse Speed and Freeze Frames
Reverse speed and freeze frames are creative effects that allow you to play with time, creating reversed motion or paused moments in your video.

- **Reverse Speed**: To reverse a clip, right-click it in the timeline and go to **Speed/Duration**, then check the **Reverse Speed** box. This will play the clip backward, often used for rewind effects or surreal motion.
- **Freeze Frame**: A freeze frame pauses a clip at a specific frame, creating a still image from the video. Right-click the clip in the timeline and choose **Add Frame Hold** or **Insert Frame Hold Segment**. This holds the image at the selected frame, useful for emphasizing specific moments.

Each of these speed and time effects in Premiere Pro gives you the flexibility to shape the pacing of your project, whether you're emphasizing certain actions, speeding up sequences, or manipulating time for creative storytelling.

Chapter 14

Multicam Editing Basics

1. Setting Up Multicam Sequences
Multicam editing allows you to combine footage from multiple cameras, making it easy to switch between different angles seamlessly. Here's how to set up a multicam sequence in Premiere Pro:

- **Importing Your Footage**: Begin by importing all the camera angles you plan to use in your sequence. Ensure each clip is clearly labeled to avoid confusion later on.
- **Creating a Multicam Sequence**: Select all the clips you want to include, right-click, and choose **Create Multi-Camera Source Sequence**. In the dialog box that appears, select your preferred sync method (audio, timecode, or in/out points). Premiere Pro will sync the clips automatically based on your selection and create the multicam sequence.
- **Setting Up the Sequence**: After generating the multicam sequence, drag it to the timeline. Premiere Pro will stack your camera angles on top of each other, with the primary angle visible by default.

2. Switching Angles
Once the multicam sequence is set up, you can switch between angles during playback:

- **Enable the Program Monitor**: Ensure the **Program Monitor** is activated and configured for multicam editing. Click the + button in the **Program Monitor** settings to add the **Multicam** view.
- **Switching Angles in Real-Time**: While playing back the sequence, simply click the corresponding camera angle in the **Program Monitor** to switch in real-time. Premiere Pro will instantly transition to the selected angle.
- **Keyboard Shortcuts for Angle Switching**: You can use the numbers 1-9 on your keyboard to quickly switch between camera angles in your multicam sequence.

3. Syncing Audio and Video
Synchronizing audio and video is vital for seamless editing, especially when using multiple cameras to capture the same event:

- **Syncing via Audio**: If your cameras recorded audio, you can sync them automatically by selecting the clips in your sequence, right-clicking, and choosing **Synchronize**. Select **Audio** as the sync method, and Premiere Pro will align the clips based on their audio waveforms.
- **Manual Syncing**: If automatic syncing doesn't work as expected, you can manually align the clips by adjusting them on the timeline. Zoom in on the audio waveforms and match the peaks visually.
- **Audio Mixdown**: Once the audio and video are synchronized, you

can mix down the audio to ensure consistent sound across all angles. Use the **Audio Track Mixer** or adjust the levels in the **Effect Controls** panel to balance the audio.

Multicam editing simplifies the process of switching between different shots, making it an invaluable technique for editing live events, interviews, performances, or any project requiring multiple perspectives. By setting up multicam sequences, efficiently switching angles, and syncing audio and video, you can produce professional-quality results quickly.

Chapter 15

Using Masks and Tracking

1. Creating and Editing Masks
Masks are key tools in Premiere Pro that enable you to isolate specific areas of a video clip, allowing for targeted application of effects or adjustments. Here's how to create and modify masks:

- **Creating a Mask:** To create a mask, select the clip you want to work on and go to the **Effect Controls** panel. In the **Opacity** section, you'll find options to create masks. You can use the **Free Draw Bezier** tool (to draw freehand), or choose the **Ellipse Mask** or **Rectangle Mask**. After selecting your mask shape, adjust it to target the desired part of the frame.

- **Editing a Mask:** After the mask is created, you can modify its shape, size, and position directly in the **Program Monitor**. Additionally, you can adjust the mask's feather (softness of the edges) and its opacity. You can also animate the mask's path over time by setting keyframes.

2. Masking for Effects and Corrections
Masks are often used to apply effects or corrections to specific areas within a clip:

- **Applying Effects to the Masked Area**: Once a mask is created, any effect applied in the **Effect Controls** panel will only affect the area within the mask. This technique is useful for tasks like color correction, applying blur effects, or making other adjustments to isolated parts of the frame.
- **Using Masks for Color Grading**: Masks are particularly beneficial for color grading. For example, if you want to adjust the color of the sky without altering the rest of the scene, you can create a mask around the sky and apply color correction exclusively to that area.
- **Using Multiple Masks**: You can use multiple masks on the same clip to apply different corrections or effects. Each mask can be adjusted independently, allowing you to combine them for more complex results.

3. Motion Tracking with Effects

Motion tracking lets you follow the movement of objects within your footage and apply effects that stay in sync with that movement. Here's how to use motion tracking in Premiere Pro:

- **Applying Motion Tracking**: To track motion, select the clip and go to the **Effect Controls** panel. Under **Opacity**, click the **Track Motion** button. Premiere Pro will display a tracking point that you can place on the object you wish to track. The software will then follow the object's movement throughout the clip.
- **Tracking an Object**: Once the tracking point is set, Premiere Pro will

track the object's movement from frame to frame. You can refine the tracking path by adjusting the position or adding keyframes if necessary.

- **Applying Effects to the Tracked Object**: After tracking the object, you can apply effects such as a blur or color correction to the tracked area. The effect will automatically follow the object's movement as it shifts in the frame.

Masks and motion tracking offer greater precision in editing by allowing you to focus on specific areas of the frame. These tools, when used effectively, can significantly elevate your video projects, whether you're isolating parts for adjustments or applying effects to moving elements within your scene.

Chapter 16

Green Screen and Compositing

1.   **Using**   **Ultra**   **Key**
The Ultra Key effect in Premiere Pro is an effective tool for removing green (or blue) screen backgrounds from video clips, a technique known as chroma keying. This process isolates the background, making it transparent and allowing you to replace it with a different scene or background.

- **Applying   Ultra   Key**:
  To use Ultra Key, drag it from the Effects panel and apply it to the clip in your timeline. In the Effect Controls panel, you'll find the Ultra Key effect. Use the Eyedropper tool to select the background color you wish to remove (typically green or blue). Premiere Pro will then make that color transparent.
- **Fine-tuning   Ultra   Key**:
  After applying the Ultra Key, adjust the settings to enhance the quality of the keying. Use the **Matte Generation** controls to tweak transparency, **Matte Cleanup** to refine the edges, and **Spill Suppression** to eliminate any residual background color on your subject.

2.   **Background**   **Replacement**
After successfully removing the green screen, you can replace it with a new background, be it an image or video, to place the subject in a completely new setting.

- **Importing a New Background**: Import your new background into the project and position it on the timeline beneath the keyed clip. Ensure the new background is appropriately sized and placed within the frame.
- **Adjusting the Subject**: You may need to adjust the subject's position, scale, or rotation to align with the new background. Use the **Motion** controls in the Effect Controls panel for adjustments. Ensure the subject's lighting and perspective match the background for a convincing composite.

3. Color Spill and Edge Refinement
While using a green screen, color spill can occur, where the background color bleeds onto the subject. Additionally, the edges of the key can appear too harsh or rough, breaking the illusion of the composite. Refining both the edges and spill is essential for achieving a polished result.

- **Managing Color Spill**: Color spill occurs when the green background reflects onto the subject, usually noticeable along the edges. To address this, use the **Spill Suppression** setting in the Ultra Key effect to remove the unwanted green color around the subject.
- **Refining the Edges**: The edges of your keyed subject might appear jagged or too harsh. To smooth this out, use the **Edge Feathering** and **Edge Thin** controls in the Ultra Key effect. Feathering softens the key's edges, helping the subject blend more naturally

with the background. You can also adjust the **Choke** setting to fine-tune how much of the keyed area is affected.

By utilizing these tools—Ultra Key, background replacement, and color spill/edge refinement—you can achieve seamless green screen compositing, allowing for realistic placement of subjects in new environments while ensuring high-quality results.

Chapter 17

Working with Captions and Subtitles

1.   Creating   and   Importing   Captions
Captions and subtitles play a crucial role in conveying dialogue and sound information in your video, helping to make it more accessible to a broader audience. Here's how you can create and import them:

- **Creating   Captions**:
  In Premiere Pro, you can create captions by going to the Captions panel. Navigate to **File > New > Captions**, then select the type of captions you need (such as Open or Closed Captions). After creating the caption file, you can manually input the text and align it with the video's timing.
- **Importing   Captions**:
  If you already have a caption file (like an SRT or SCC file), importing it into Premiere Pro is straightforward. Simply go to **File > Import**, select the caption file, and Premiere Pro will add it to your timeline as a caption track.

2.   Styling   and   Syncing   Text
Once the captions are created or imported, you can modify their appearance and ensure they sync properly with the video:

- **Styling   Captions**:
  Use the **Essential Graphics** panel to adjust the
  look of your captions. You can change the font,
  size,   color,   background,   and   placement.
  Customizing the captions' style ensures they
  blend seamlessly with your video's overall design
  and are easy to read.
- **Syncing   Captions   with   Video**:
  It's important to synchronize the captions with the
  video accurately. You can manually adjust the
  timing by dragging the caption blocks in the
  timeline to match the spoken words or sound cues.
  Additionally, Premiere Pro allows you to modify
  the duration of each caption to ensure proper
  pacing.

3.   Exporting   Videos   with   Subtitles
Once you've worked with captions and subtitles, the next
step is exporting the video along with the text:

- **Embedding   Subtitles**:
  You have the option to embed subtitles directly
  into the video, making them visible throughout.
  To do this, go to **File > Export > Media**, then
  select the option to include captions in the export
  settings. You can either burn the captions into the
  video or export them as a separate file, depending
  on your needs.
- **Exporting   as   a   Separate   File**:
  If you prefer to keep the captions as a separate file
  (like an SRT), you can choose to export them
  alongside the video, allowing viewers to toggle
  the subtitles on or off as needed.

By effectively creating, styling, syncing, and exporting captions and subtitles, you improve your video's accessibility, making it more engaging for a diverse audience while ensuring clarity and understanding.

Chapter 18

Collaborating and Sharing Projects

1.   Using   Team   Projects
Team Projects in Premiere Pro allow multiple users to work together on a single project from anywhere. This feature lets editors collaborate in real-time, working on different sections of the same project simultaneously. It's particularly beneficial for teams working remotely or in different time zones, offering seamless teamwork with cloud synchronization, version tracking, and shared resources.

2.   Sharing   Media   and   Timelines
Sharing media and timelines is crucial for effective collaboration in a team setting. You can share project files, media, and sequences by using shared storage or cloud services, ensuring all team members have access to the same materials. This enables everyone to work on their respective tasks without version issues. Premiere Pro also supports sharing entire timelines, which makes it easier to collaborate on edits, color grading, or sound design while maintaining consistent content across all team members.

3.   Version   Control   and   Autosave
Version control keeps a record of project changes, allowing you to track edits and revert to previous versions

when needed. Premiere Pro includes a version history feature that allows you to save different project versions as you progress. Autosave is another helpful tool that automatically saves your work at set intervals, minimizing the risk of losing progress. If your system crashes, you can recover the most recent autosave and resume editing without significant interruptions.

By using Team Projects, sharing media and timelines, and taking advantage of version control and autosave, you can improve collaboration and streamline the editing process, especially when working with a team. These features ensure smooth coordination and efficiency, even when collaborating remotely.

Chapter 19

Exporting Your Final Video

Using the Export Settings Panel

The Export Settings panel in Premiere Pro allows you to adjust the parameters for rendering and exporting your project. It provides the flexibility to customize settings for various platforms, formats, and resolutions. Here's how to navigate and use the Export Settings panel effectively:

1. **Opening the Export Settings Panel**
   After completing your video edits, go to **File > Export > Media** to open the Export Settings panel. This is where you'll configure the export settings for your final output.

2. **Selecting the Format**
   The first option in the Export Settings panel is the **Format** dropdown. You can choose from various formats like **H.264**, **QuickTime**, or **Apple ProRes** based on your needs. **H.264** is ideal for web-based videos, while **QuickTime** or **ProRes** are used for professional or high-quality outputs.

3. **Choosing a Preset**
   Under the **Format** option, you can select a **Preset**. These are predefined settings tailored for specific platforms or devices, such as **YouTube 1080p** or **Vimeo 4K**. Selecting a preset automatically adjusts the resolution, frame rate, and other settings to suit your intended output.

4. **Configuring Output Parameters**

- **Resolution**: Set the resolution to match the platform you're exporting for, such as 1920x1080 for Full HD or 3840x2160 for 4K.
- **Frame Rate**: Make sure the frame rate aligns with your project settings or the platform's requirements. Common options are 24fps, 30fps, or 60fps.
- **Bitrate**: The bitrate affects the video's quality and file size. Higher bitrates provide better quality but result in larger files. Adjust this based on the importance of file size for your project.

5. **Audio   Settings**
   You can adjust the audio settings in the Export Settings panel. Choose the appropriate audio codec, sample rate, bitrate, and channel configuration (stereo or mono). AAC is typically used for audio, with a 48 kHz sample rate being standard for most exports.

6. **Enabling   Maximum   Render   Quality**
   For the highest quality output, enable the **Use Maximum Render Quality** option. While this may increase export time, it enhances the final result, especially when scaling video resolution.

7. **Queue   vs.   Export**
   You have the option to either send your export to the **Queue** (using Adobe Media Encoder) or export directly from Premiere Pro. Using the **Queue** is helpful for batch processing multiple exports, saving time if you have several projects to render.

8. **Exporting   the   Video**
   Once you're happy with your settings, click **Export** to start rendering your video. If you used the **Queue**, it will appear in Adobe Media Encoder, where you can initiate the export process from there.

Understanding Video Formats and Codecs

In video production and editing, it's essential to grasp the distinction between formats and codecs, as they significantly influence the quality and size of your exports. Here's a detailed look at both and their role in your video work:

1. Video Formats

A video **format** is the container that holds your video and audio data, along with metadata and additional components like subtitles. It defines how the video and audio streams are packaged, ensuring compatibility across different devices and software.

Popular Video Formats:

- **MP4 (H.264)**: A widely used format that provides great quality with relatively small file sizes, perfect for web streaming, social media, and general distribution.
- **MOV (QuickTime)**: Typically used for professional video editing, especially on Apple devices. It supports high-quality codecs like ProRes.

- **AVI (Audio Video Interleave)**: A Microsoft-developed format that supports multiple codecs but tends to generate large files with less compression.
- **MKV (Matroska)**: A versatile format that can store various types of video, audio, and subtitle tracks. It's popular for HD content but may lack support on some platforms.
- **WMV (Windows Media Video)**: A Microsoft format, primarily used on Windows systems, but not universally supported.
- **FLV (Flash Video)**: Previously used for online streaming, FLV has become less popular as Flash technology has declined.

2. Codecs

A **codec** (compressor-decompressor) is used to compress or encode video and audio data for storage or transmission. It also decodes the data for playback. Different codecs offer varying trade-offs between file size, quality, and compatibility.

Common Video Codecs:

- **H.264**: The most popular video codec for streaming, offering a good balance of quality and file size. It's supported across most devices and platforms.
- **H.265 (HEVC)**: The successor to H.264, H.265 achieves the same video quality at half the file size, making it ideal for 4K or high-definition content, though it may not be as widely supported.

- **ProRes**: Developed by Apple, ProRes is a high-quality codec favored in professional video editing. It preserves more detail than H.264 and is commonly used in film production. There are different ProRes variants, such as ProRes 422 and ProRes 4444, offering varying levels of compression and quality.
- **VP9**: A Google-developed codec used for YouTube and other streaming services, offering similar efficiency to H.265 but with open-source licensing.
- **AV1**: A newer open-source codec designed for better compression than HEVC, mainly used in newer streaming services.

Common Audio Codecs:

- **AAC (Advanced Audio Codec)**: Often used for streaming and consumer video, offering a good balance of quality and file size.
- **MP3**: Commonly used for audio compression, especially in music, but less efficient than AAC for video.
- **WAV**: An uncompressed audio format that delivers the highest quality, but results in larger file sizes.
- **FLAC (Free Lossless Audio Codec)**: A lossless audio codec that compresses audio without sacrificing quality, popular in high-fidelity audio systems.

3. How Formats and Codecs Work Together

A video file is typically made up of a **format** (container) that holds both video and audio streams, which are encoded using specific **codecs**. For example:

- **MP4 (Format)** may use **H.264 (Codec)** for video and **AAC (Codec)** for audio.
- **MOV (Format)** might use **ProRes (Codec)** for video and **PCM (Codec)** for audio.

While the format dictates how the file is structured, the codec determines how the video and audio are compressed and their quality. Choosing the appropriate format and codec should be based on the video's intended use, considering compatibility, quality, and file size.

4. Choosing the Right Format and Codec

- For **web streaming or social media**, **H.264 in MP4** is usually the best choice due to its efficient balance between quality and file size.
- For **professional editing and archiving, ProRes or DNxHD** in **MOV** or **MXF** formats provides high quality and more editing flexibility.
- For **high-definition and 4K web video, H.265 in MP4** is ideal for smaller file sizes without sacrificing quality.
- For **audio-only projects**, **AAC or MP3** provides a great balance of size and quality.

Export Presets for YouTube, Instagram, and More

When exporting videos for various platforms, it's crucial to select the appropriate settings to optimize the content according to each platform's specifications. Premiere Pro offers export presets designed for common platforms like YouTube, Instagram, Vimeo, and others. Here's an overview of the most popular presets for different platforms:

1. YouTube Presets

YouTube is a top video-sharing platform, with specific requirements to ensure your video looks great and maintains a manageable file size.

- **YouTube 1080p Full HD**: This preset is perfect for uploading HD videos (1920x1080 resolution). It uses the H.264 codec for compression, balancing quality and file size, with the AAC codec typically used for audio.
- **YouTube 4K Ultra HD**: For 4K videos, this preset exports at **3840x2160 resolution** and uses the H.265/HEVC codec for efficient high-resolution compression.
- **YouTube 720p HD**: This preset offers a more compressed version of your video, exporting at **1280x720 resolution** for smaller file sizes.

2. Instagram Presets

Instagram videos are viewed primarily on mobile devices, so it's important to choose settings that align with the platform's aspect ratio and resolution.

- **Instagram Square Video (1:1 aspect ratio)**: This preset creates square videos for Instagram's main feed, with a recommended resolution of **1080x1080**.

- **Instagram Portrait Video (4:5 aspect ratio)**: For taller videos, this preset exports at **1080x1350 resolution**, ideal for utilizing vertical screen space on mobile.
- **Instagram Landscape Video (16:9 aspect ratio)**: This preset, which exports at **1920x1080 resolution**, is perfect for landscape videos that maintain high-quality formatting.

3. Facebook Presets

Facebook supports various video formats, and selecting the right export settings can enhance the video quality.

- **Facebook 1080p HD**: This preset exports at **1920x1080 resolution** using the H.264 codec, optimized for Facebook's video specifications.
- **Facebook 720p HD**: For quicker uploads and smaller file sizes, this preset exports at **1280x720 resolution**, making it more suitable for mobile-friendly content.

4. Vimeo Presets

Vimeo is renowned for supporting high-quality videos, making it a preferred platform for professionals and filmmakers.

- **Vimeo 1080p HD**: Like YouTube's 1080p preset, this setting exports at **1920x1080 resolution** using the H.264 codec for video and AAC codec for audio to ensure top-quality results.
- **Vimeo 4K Ultra HD**: This preset supports 4K videos at **3840x2160 resolution**, utilizing the

H.265/HEVC codec for effective compression and quality retention.

5. Other Common Platforms

- **Twitter**: To optimize videos for Twitter, use a **1080p resolution** (1920x1080) with **H.264 codec** and **AAC audio**, which is ideal for fast mobile loading.
- **TikTok**: TikTok videos are usually in portrait mode, and you'll want to use the **9:16 aspect ratio** (1080x1920 resolution). Exporting with **H.264 codec** for video and **AAC codec** for audio ensures compatibility with TikTok's mobile-first approach.

How to Use Presets in Premiere Pro

To use a preset in Premiere Pro:

1. Go to **File > Export > Media**.
2. In the **Export Settings** panel, select the appropriate format from the **Format** dropdown (e.g., H.264).
3. Below the format, choose the corresponding **Preset** for the platform (e.g., YouTube 1080p, Instagram 1:1).
4. Premiere Pro will automatically adjust the settings, including resolution and frame rate, based on your selected preset.

Chapter 20

Troubleshooting Common Issues

Fixing   Playback   and   Lag
Playback problems and lag can interfere with your editing, causing slowdowns and frustration. Here are some solutions to address these issues:

- **Adjust Playback Settings**: To reduce the strain on your system, lower the playback resolution in the program monitor to 1/2 or 1/4.
- **Use Proxy Files**: For high-resolution content, use proxy files to ensure smoother playback. Proxies are lower-resolution versions that can be swapped with full-resolution clips during export.
- **Update Drivers and Software**: Keep your graphics drivers and Premiere Pro updated, as outdated software can lead to lag and poor performance.
- **Clear Cache**: Premiere Pro stores cache files that can slow down performance over time. Clear them through **Preferences > Media Cache** to improve playback.

Relinking   Offline   Media
Offline media occurs when Premiere Pro can no longer locate the original files linked to your project. Here's how to fix it:

- **Find Missing Files**: If a file is missing, Premiere Pro will mark it as offline. Right-click the offline clip in the timeline or Project panel and select **Link Media.**

- **Locate the File**: Navigate to the location of the original file, select it, and click **OK** to relink the media to your project.
- **Relink Multiple Files**: If multiple files are offline, select all the offline files in the Project panel, right-click, and choose **Link Media.** Premiere Pro will ask you to locate the folder with the missing files and relink them all at once.

Error   Messages   and   Crashes
If Premiere Pro shows error messages or crashes unexpectedly, here's how to troubleshoot:

- **Verify System Requirements**: Check that your system meets Premiere Pro's minimum hardware and software specifications. Lack of memory or processing power may cause crashes.
- **Reset Preferences**: Corrupted preferences can cause issues. To reset them, hold **Alt (Option on Mac)** while launching Premiere Pro.
- **Update the Software**: Ensure you're using the latest version of Premiere Pro, as updates often resolve bugs and enhance stability.
- **Disable Conflicting Plugins**: Third-party plugins can sometimes cause issues. Disable or remove recently added plugins to see if that fixes the problem.
- **Investigate Error Codes**: When an error code appears, take note of it and search online for potential solutions.

Chapter 21

Keyboard Shortcuts and Time-Saving Tips

Essential Editing Shortcuts
Using keyboard shortcuts can significantly speed up your editing workflow by allowing you to execute commands quickly without needing to navigate menus. Below are some key editing shortcuts in Premiere Pro:

- **Play/Pause**: Spacebar
- **Undo**: Ctrl+Z (Windows) / Cmd+Z (Mac)
- **Redo**: Ctrl+Shift+Z (Windows) / Cmd+Shift+Z (Mac)
- **Cut**: Ctrl+K (Windows) / Cmd+K (Mac)
- **Ripple Delete**: Shift+Delete (Windows) / Shift+Backspace (Mac)
- **Zoom In/Out on Timeline**: + / -
- **Select All**: Ctrl+A (Windows) / Cmd+A (Mac)
- **Add Edit**: Ctrl+Shift+K (Windows) / Cmd+Shift+K (Mac)
- **Toggle Audio Scrubbing**: Shift+S
- **Toggle Video Track Output**: Shift+1-9 (for toggling specific tracks)

Customizing Keyboard Layout
You can personalize your keyboard shortcuts in Premiere Pro to better suit your editing style. Here's how to customize them:

1. Go to **Edit > Keyboard Shortcuts** (Windows) or **Premiere Pro > Keyboard Shortcuts** (Mac).
2. In the shortcuts panel, search for commands by name or browse through categories.
3. Select the shortcut you want to modify and press the new key combination.
4. You can save your custom shortcuts as a preset.
5. If you wish to revert to the default settings, simply click **Reset to Default**.

Speeding   Up   Your   Workflow
To improve your efficiency and speed up your editing process in Premiere Pro, try these helpful tips:

- **Use Nested Sequences**: Nest sequences when dealing with complex projects to simplify the timeline and make edits easier to manage.
- **Work with Multiple Monitors**: Expand your editing space by using multiple monitors for the Program and Source panels, giving you a better overview of your work.
- **Utilize the Media Browser**: Rather than manually importing files, use the Media Browser to quickly locate and import your clips directly into your project.
- **Use Adjustment Layers**: Apply effects across multiple clips simultaneously by using adjustment layers, which saves time on global adjustments.
- **Organize Projects with Bins**: Keep your project organized by sorting assets into bins. This helps you quickly locate files and improves your workflow.

- **Enable Auto Save**: Ensure auto-save is activated to protect your progress in case Premiere Pro crashes unexpectedly.

Chapter 22

Next Steps and Advancing Your Skills

Free   Resources   and   Tutorials
There are many free resources to help you continue improving your editing skills, including tutorials, courses, and online communities. Here are some key options:

- **Adobe's Official Website**: Adobe offers in-depth tutorials, covering everything from basic editing techniques to advanced Premiere Pro features.
- **YouTube Tutorials**: Many professional editors provide valuable tips and tutorials on YouTube, offering step-by-step guides and editing workflow enhancements.
- **Online Learning Platforms**: Platforms like Skillshare, LinkedIn Learning, and Coursera provide free or trial-based courses on video editing and Premiere Pro.
- **Forums and Blogs**: Participating in forums like the Adobe Community or following video editing blogs can help you gain insights from others' experiences and discover new editing techniques.

Joining   the   Adobe   Community
Becoming part of the Adobe community is a great way to

stay updated and continue learning about video editing. By connecting with others, you can:

- Share your projects and receive constructive feedback.
- Engage in discussions on tips, tricks, and troubleshooting.
- Join Adobe user groups, attend webinars, and follow Adobe's social media channels to keep up with the latest features and updates.
- Collaborate with other creators to share knowledge and ideas.

Advancing to the Intermediate Level
To progress to the intermediate level of video editing, focus on mastering advanced features in Premiere Pro:

- **Advanced Color Grading**: Learn how to use tools like the Lumetri Color panel for detailed color correction and creative grading.
- **Multicam Editing**: Dive into multicam editing to seamlessly edit multiple camera angles simultaneously.
- **Audio Editing**: Expand your knowledge of audio editing by mastering tools like the Essential Sound panel and other key audio effects.
- **Motion Graphics and Animation**: Explore Adobe After Effects to create high-quality animations and motion graphics that integrate with your Premiere Pro projects.
- **Keyboard Shortcuts and Workflow Efficiency**: Optimize your workflow by mastering advanced keyboard shortcuts, automation features, and

panel customizations to streamline your editing process.